spy, n. — a secret agent employed by a government or other organization
to gather intelligence relating to its actual or potential enemies

М. П.
должность, звание и подпись командира части
(начальника учреждения), выдавшего удосто
верение
27 Июня 19
Серия
УДО
Л
1. Предъяви
состоит
службе

Spies around the World

AND OTHER RUSSIAN SPIES

Michael E. Goodman

CREATIVE EDUCATION

A man is arrested in 1950 for giving the Russians information about the atomic bomb.

Table of Contents

Chapters

- -

Evolution of Espionage

- -

Published by Creative Education
P.O. Box 227, Mankato, Minnesota 56002
Creative Education is an imprint of
The Creative Company
www.thecreativecompany.us

Design and production by Blue Design
Art direction by Rita Marshall
Printed in the United States of America

Photographs by Getty Images (Jeffrey Coolidge,
Ralph Crane/Time Life Pictures, DON EMMERT/AFP,
Evening Standard, LUKE FRAZZA/AFP, Bob Gomel//
Time Life Pictures, Hulton Archive, Keystone/Hulton
Archive, Keystone-France/Gamma-Keystone, Laski
Collection, Laski Diffusion, Will & Deni McIntyre,
Sasha Mordovets, Carl Mydans//Time Life Pictures,
Popperfoto, Walter Sanders/Time & Life Pictures,
Universal History Archive, Bill Wallace/NY Daily News
Archive, Konstantin Zavrazhin), NASA

Library of Congress Cataloging-in-Publication Data
Goodman, Michael E.
The KGB and other Russian spies / by Michael E.
Goodman.
p. cm. — (Spies around the world)
Includes bibliographical references and index.
Summary: An eye-opening exploration of the history
of the 1954-founded KGB and other Russian espionage
agencies, investigating their typical training and
tools as well as the escapades of famous spies.
ISBN 978-1-60818-227-5
1. Intelligence service—Soviet Union—Juvenile
literature. 2. Soviet Union. Komitet gosudarstvennoi
bezopasnosti—Juvenile literature. 3. Espionage,
Soviet—Juvenile literature. 4. Spies—Soviet Union—
Juvenile literature. I. Title.

JN6529.I6G67 2012
327.1247—dc23   2011035790

CPSIA: 102212 PO1612

9 8 7 6 5 4 3 2

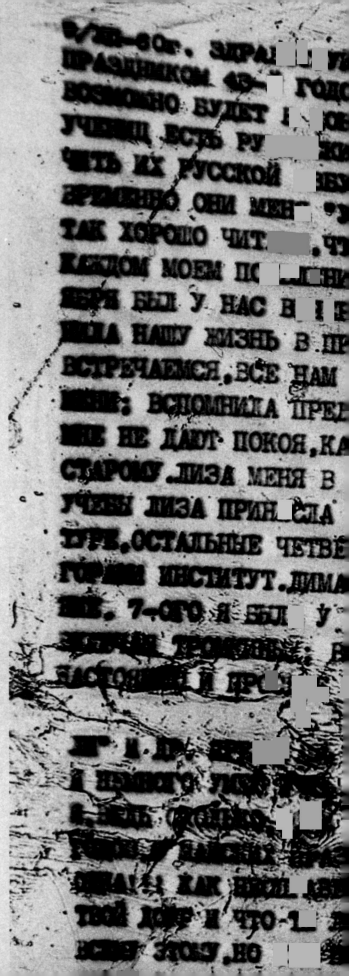

...РОГ... И ХОРОШИЙ МОЙ! ПОЗДРАВЛЯЮ... ВСЕХ С ПРОШ...
...Й ОКТЯБРЯ.ЖДАЛИ ОТ ТЕБЯ ПИСЬМА,НО ОКАЗАЛОСЬ...
...СИНЕ. НА РАБОТЕ У МЕНЯ ВСЕ ХОРОШО.СРЕДИ...
...ДЕВОЧКИ 7 И 8 ЛЕТ.И ВОТ Я ВЗЯЛА НА СЕБЯ 3...
...УСПЕХИ КОЛОССАЛЬНЫЕ (КОНЕЧНО,ЗАСЛУГИ ДЕВОЧЕК)...
...РУМЫНСКОМУ. ПРИ ОБХОДЕ ШКОЛЫ С КОМИССИЕЙ ШК ОНИ
...НЕ КАК-ТО ХОРОШО И ПРИЯТНО СТАЛО НА ДУШЕ,ТЕПЕРЬ...
...ОНИ МЕНЯ СПРАШИВАЮТ,А БУДУ ЛИ Я ИХ УЧИТЬ ЕЩЕ?!! Я
...А РАБОТЕ,НА КОТОРОМ Я ПЕЛА "ЖУРАВЛИ" И ПРОЧЕЕ.ЕСЛ...
...Е И К К-ТО СТАЛО ГРУСТНО-ГРУСТНО, ВЕДЬ СКОЛЬКО Ж...
...ОДИТСЯ КУДА-ТО СПЕШИТЬ И ВСЕ У НАС НЕ ХВАТАЕТ...
...ЛЕДНИЙ ДЕНЬ,ПРОВЕДЕННЫЙ В ПРАГЕ.А ОСОБЕННО ЖУРАВ...
...ТО ТЯ ЕЛО И ГРУСТНО СТАЛО ИХ ПЕТЬ. ДОМА У НАС В...
...Й ЧЕТВЕРТИ ОЧЕНЬ ОГОРЧИЛА.ПЕРВЫЙ РАЗ ЗА ШЕСТЬ ЛЕТ
...ТРОЙКИ...ПО ГЕОМЕТРИИ,АЛГЕБРЕ,АНГЛИЙСКОМУ И СКОЛЬ
...ТЫ НЕ ПРЕДСТАВЛЯЕШЬ,КАК Я РАССТРОИЛАСЬ.ВЕДЬ НЕ З
...ИНЕС ЕЩЕ ХУЖЕ ОТМЕТКИ,ВКЛЮЧАЯ ДИСЦИПЛИНУ И ПРОЧ...
...Ы И ИГОРЯ,ВЕЧЕР ПРОШЕЛ ОЧЕНЬ ХОРОШО.БЫЛО 14 ЧЕЛОВ...
...ЛИ ЗА ТЕБЯ,ВСЕ ТЕБЯ ВСПОМИНАЮТ ДОБРЫМИ СЛОВАМИ. НО
...НЫ И ВСЕХ ПРИСУТСТВУЮЩИХ.Я СПЕЛА-ОПЯТЬ-ТАКИ "ЖУРА...

...Е.ПРОИЗВЕЛА ВПЕЧАТЛЕНИЕ НА ВСЕХ,НИКТО НЕ ДУМАЛ,ЧТО
...МЫ ОЧЕНЬ ОГОРЧИЛИСЬ,ЧТО НЕ БЫЛО ТЕБЯ,А ОСОБЕННО
...ЖИВЕТ. МНЕ ПАМЯТЬ,ТО УЖЕ 7 ОКТЯБРЬСКИХ И 6 НОВЫХ
...ОВ-ЭТО НЕ ВКЛЮЧАЯ ПРОЧИХ ФАМИЛЬНЫХ ТОРЖЕСТВ.Я
...ЖИЗНЬ. Я ВСЕ ПОНИ...
...ЧТО ЭТО
...Ы СВОЮ РАБОТУ И ОЧЕНЬ ДОБРОСОВЕСТНО ОТНОСИШЬСЯ КО
...БЕ. Я КАК-ТО ЧИСТО ПО-ОБЫВАТЕЛЬСКИ РАССУЖДАЮ С...

In 1565, the ruthless Russian tsar Ivan the Terrible created a 6,000-member security force called the Oprichnina. Officers of the Oprichnina dressed all in black and rode black horses. They terrified and terrorized the Russian people, killing thousands whom they blamed for made-up acts of treason. Many rulers after Ivan also created their own security forces to spy on Russians at home or living outside the country. The Russian security forces of the 20th and 21st centuries—known at different times as the Cheka, NKVD, KGB, and SVR—have added to a long tradition of power, fear, and secrecy that began more than 400 years ago.

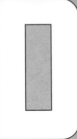
REVOLUTION AND ESPIONAGE

During the 20th century, perhaps no country in the world went through more dramatic changes than Russia. In 1917, the Russian Revolution ended rule by tsars in the country. The revolution was followed by a bloody civil war and the establishment of a new kind of dictatorship. In 1922, the country was renamed the Union of Soviet Socialist Republics (USSR), or Soviet Union for short. Two years later, Vladimir Lenin, the admired leader of the revolution, died. He was replaced by Joseph Stalin, a man who was both cruel and suspicious of everyone around him. Under Stalin, the USSR expanded, taking control of many Eastern European countries. Stalin terrorized the people under his rule until his death in 1953. The Soviet Union was then controlled by a series of communist leaders until economic problems led to another kind of revolution. In 1991, the Soviet Union was disbanded, and the different republics that had made up the confederation became independent states. The largest of those states retained the name

Russia and established a more open economic system.

Prior to the breakup of the Soviet Union, struggles for power had been constant. Soviet leaders feared that citizens who had left the country might plot to overthrow the communist government. To help maintain control, Soviet leaders followed the tradition established by Ivan the Terrible, setting up spy agencies. These agencies had two main purposes—ensuring that people inside the country were not plotting against the government (counterespionage) and uncovering information on activities in other nations that might pose a threat to

the Soviet Union (espionage).

The first spy organization that Lenin established in 1917 was called the Cheka (Extraordinary Commission for Combating Counterrevolution and Sabotage). It was headed by Felix Dzerzhinsky, a remarkable spy and con man. Dzerzhinsky's greatest achievement was setting up a fictitious anti-communist organization called "the Trust." His agents persuaded several foreign intelligence organizations to invest money in the Trust, believing it would help overthrow the communists. Lenin's government used that money for its own purposes. A number

Right: Vladimir Lenin was famous for the speeches he directed to working-class Russians.

EVOLUTION OF ESPIONAGE
Sneaky and Sinister

After the assassination of Tsar Alexander II in 1881, his successor, Alexander III, took steps to crack down on possible rebels. Following a long Russian tradition, the tsar established a secret police force and intelligence organization he called the Okhrana to keep track of any enemies to the crown. One of the Okhrana's main techniques involved placing agents undercover inside groups of dissidents. The agents not only kept track of what the rebels were planning, but they also often pushed them into carrying out illegal acts. Most often, the dissidents were quickly arrested and exiled to a frigid wilderness area in eastern Russia called Siberia.

of Russian leaders in exile and anti-communist spies were also persuaded to join the Trust. Most were soon arrested or killed.

Stalin came to power in 1922, and soon after, the spy agency was renamed the OGPU (Unified State Political Administration). He also gave it the new mission of ridding the country of landowning farmers who did not want to come under the communist system. Farms were taken away from such families. Those who objected were exiled to remote places such as Siberia or killed.

In the 1930s, the OGPU became part of the NKVD (People's Commissariat for Internal Affairs), and its duties were expanded. The NKVD not only handled espionage activities, but it also oversaw the country's police force, border patrols, criminal investigation units, domestic armed forces, and prison system. Using the NKVD, Stalin set up a police state that tried to control what everyone in the country said, did, or thought. NKVD agents weeded out any dissidents, who were then imprisoned or killed. Even many of the men who had joined Lenin and Stalin in the Russian Revolution were rounded up and executed.

At the onset of World War II (1939–45), the NKVD expanded Soviet spying activities into other countries, particularly the United States and Great Britain. Soviet leaders were worried that capitalist countries (which believed in free trade and private ownership of all property) would try to undermine their communist regime. A major effort was undertaken to convince American and British citizens, including intelligence officers of both countries, to spy for the Soviet Union. In fact, a number of high-ranking intelligence officers did become double agents. They provided the Soviet Union with key information about British and American espionage activities and revealed the identities of many operatives spying inside the USSR.

The recruiting effort in America accelerated once the U.S. began developing atomic bombs in the mid-1940s. Soviet leaders felt their country must also have nuclear weapons to compete against the U.S. The push to uncover nuclear

Alexander III enacted many policies intended to unify Russia but which led to revolution.

Above: Felix Dzerzhinsky (middle) became known as "Iron Felix" for his ruthless cunning.

secrets was the start of a 46-year competition (1945–91) between the U.S. and USSR that became known as the Cold War.

After Stalin died in 1953, Georgy Malenkov took control and oversaw the 1954 creation of a new spy agency, the KGB (Committee for State Security). The KGB was even more intent than the NKVD had been on controlling everything that went on inside the country. At one time, the KGB was believed to employ as many as 700,000 people both inside and outside the Soviet Union. Everyone living in the USSR or visiting the country came under careful KGB surveillance.

The KGB was organized into a series of 17 divisions called directorates. The First Chief Directorate handled foreign intelligence and placed agents in countries throughout the world. (Intelligence agencies in foreign countries assumed that nearly all Soviet embassy personnel stationed abroad spent at least part of their time spying for the KGB.) The Second Chief Directorate oversaw counterintelligence operations inside the USSR in much the same way as the Federal Bureau of Investigation (FBI) does in the U.S. Other directorates were responsible for military security, internal security and the fighting

EVOLUTION OF ESPIONAGE
Don't Trust the Trust

Russian-born British agent Sidney Reilly was nicknamed the "Ace of Spies." According to legend, he moved around the world spying for Great Britain and even infiltrated the German high command during World War I (1914-18). Soon after the Russian Revolution, Reilly volunteered to go to Moscow to assassinate Lenin. That plan didn't work out, and Reilly barely escaped back to London, where he continued to work against Russian communists. In 1925, Reilly was tricked into going to Moscow by representatives of "the Trust," the make-believe anti-communist organization formed by Cheka head Felix Dzerzhinsky. Once there, he was captured and killed.

of terrorism, and the monitoring of foreign communications.

The KGB (and its successor) is the organization that is portrayed in most movies or television shows that feature Russian spies, from James Bond films such as 1963's *From Russia with Love* to the television series *24* in the 2000s. In the Bond books and movies, the KGB is sometimes referred to as "SMERSH," which is believed to be an acronym for a Russian expression meaning "death to [foreign] spies."

The KGB itself came to an end in 1991 when heads of the organization tried to overthrow Russian leader Mikhail Gorbachev. The effort failed, and Gorbachev

ordered the KGB to be dismantled. It was replaced by several less powerful intelligence agencies, and staff size was cut nearly in half. The agency that took over the gathering of foreign intelligence—and continues to fulfill that role today—was the SVR (Foreign Intelligence Service). A second organization, the FSB (Federal Security Service), was established to handle internal security, police operations, and counterespionage. Although the KGB is gone, several of Russia's leaders since 1991 have been former KGB chiefs, including the current prime minister, Vladimir Putin, and the agency's infamous legacy lives on.

EVOLUTION OF ESPIONAGE
Ukraine Massacre

During the early 1930s, Stalin used the OGPU to terrorize farmers in the Ukraine (then a republic in the southwestern USSR). These farmers, called kulaks, wanted to maintain ownership of their land and crops. Stalin saw them as enemies of the communist state. OGPU agents encouraged Ukrainian peasants to expose any anti-communist farmers, who were then rounded up. Millions were executed or placed onto railroad cattle cars and shipped to Siberia. Millions more died during a severe famine. It is perhaps fitting that the OGPU leader responsible for so many deaths, Vyacheslav Menzhinsky, died violently himself when he was poisoned by a deputy who wanted his job.

Joseph Stalin forced collective farming on Soviets, claiming it would boost agricultural production.

LIVING A SPY'S LIFE

What was life like for a KGB agent? It was probably not as exciting as movies and television would lead you to believe. The Russian spies you see on the screen are often nasty villains armed with sinister weapons. While some KGB operatives may have fit that description, most did not. After all, evil-acting Russian spies would be easy for security agents in a foreign country to spot and arrest. In reality, most KGB spies looked and dressed like average people. They tried to blend in, even if they had Russian accents that made them stand out somewhat. The same goal of blending in remains true for SVR agents today.

Only a small percentage of KGB agents actually did undercover spy work themselves, such as eavesdropping on conversations, breaking into safes to steal secret documents, or taking on enemy agents in hand-to-hand combat. For most, their main job was to recruit assets—in the form

of citizens, scientists, or intelligence officers in the countries in which they served—to gather information for the Soviet Union. They would then relay the information to their bosses and give payments to the local agents. In spy talk, a person in this role is called a handler.

Spies working for the KGB fell into two categories: legals and illegals. Legals worked under their own names in a foreign country, usually for the Soviet embassy or for a Russian news agency. If they were caught spying, they would usually be arrested and deported. Illegals, on the other hand, used made-up names and identities and often worked undercover. If caught spying, they could be imprisoned for a long time or even executed. Two types of illegals often used by the KGB were moles and sleepers. Moles worked underground, or in hiding, often with an enemy's intelligence service or in a top-secret laboratory or military base. They would sneak out confidential data and turn it over during secret meetings with their handlers. A sleeper was someone with a Russian connection who was given a new identity in a foreign country. Sleepers lived ordinary lives in their new country but might be asked to spy under certain circumstances.

The life of a KGB agent could be

Opposite: Many Americans were arrested in the 1950s for passing along secrets to the KGB.

EVOLUTION OF ESPIONAGE
Scary Spies in the Sky

When the Soviet Union launched *Sputnik*, the first man-made satellite, in 1957, its plan was to experiment with a new way of spying on other countries. An underlying purpose of the launch was perhaps to intimidate Americans. While viewing film footage of the large rocket that propelled the small satellite into space, many Americans became convinced that a nuclear attack might soon be launched. Couldn't such a rocket carry nuclear weapons to the U.S., they reasoned? Although that would not have been possible, Soviet leader Nikita Khrushchev left the possibility open. "We simply switch the warhead," he boasted.

dangerous and nerve-racking. They were constantly at risk of being discovered and prosecuted. They sensed additional pressure from their own bosses. Just as Russian citizens and foreigners visiting the Soviet Union were watched closely by KGB agents, KGB spies based in foreign countries were always under observation by higher-ups to make sure they did not defect or become double agents who would reveal secrets to the enemy.

So why did people choose to join the KGB? In general, KGB agents and their families lived better lives in nicer homes and received higher wages than average Soviet citizens. After all, the government wanted to give them incentives to take such a risky job. They also were given high military ranks that improved their social

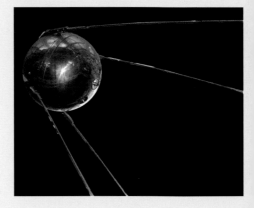

status. Recruits were especially attracted to the KGB's First Chief Directorate, the foreign intelligence corps. Members of that directorate were able to live in a foreign country and enjoy luxuries not often available in the Soviet Union.

What did the KGB look for when recruiting First Chief Directorate operatives? Most were graduates of respected colleges and universities in the USSR. Applicants with science and engineering degrees were especially desirable. Recruits also were expected to speak one or more foreign languages fluently. They were put through a two-year training program at the KGB's Red Banner Institute, located near Moscow. The curriculum included the use of ciphers (codes), training in martial arts, and lessons in how to use explosives or other methods

Above: *Sputnik* **spent three months in Earth orbit before falling back into the atmosphere.**

Several newspapers reported that the Soviet Union had tested a nuclear weapon in 1949.

Below: Aldrich Ames first appeared before a court on espionage charges on February 22, 1994.

for sabotaging military and technical equipment—skills collectively called tradecraft. Recruits also took courses in communist history and economics that further instilled the communist worldview in their minds. They received additional training in foreign languages, laws, and customs to help them keep their cover while on assignment.

Despite the training and incentives, not all KGB agents were happy in their work. The story of KGB Major Gennadi Varenik demonstrates some of the problems and temptations that Russian agents faced in foreign countries. Varenik, whose father had also worked for the KGB, was stationed in Bonn, Germany, in the 1980s. He spent a year in the offices of the Soviet news agency TASS to build his cover as a journalist. Once in Germany, he was introduced to an American spy from the Central Intelligence Agency (CIA). Each man tried unsuccessfully to recruit the other as a double agent. Then, a few years later, Varenik found himself in trouble. Tempted by the good life in Germany, Varenik had overspent his KGB salary. He had used funds from his office budget for personal expenses and was afraid of being found out. He was also concerned that one of the local spies he had recruited was really a German agent who had been providing

Varenik with disinformation, which he had relayed to Moscow. What could he do?

In March 1985, Varenik contacted his CIA "friend" and agreed to spy for the U.S. For $3,000 a month, he provided important information about the work of KGB operatives in Germany. Whenever Varenik wanted to meet his CIA contact, he would make a chalk mark on a telephone pole near the TASS office. This process went on for seven months. Then, Varenik received a message telling him to return with his family to Moscow to discuss a new assignment. He didn't have time to alert the CIA before he was hustled back to Russia. When no chalk marks showed up in Bonn for several weeks, the Americans suspected that there was a problem.

It turned out that Varenik's identity as a double agent had been revealed by an American CIA officer named Aldrich Ames, who had long been acting as a double agent for the Soviets. When Varenik returned to Moscow, he was arrested, tried for treason, and executed. Nine years later, Ames himself would be sentenced—but not before he had caused the deaths of several other double agents working for the Americans.

TOOLS OF THE TRADE

Part of the fun and excitement of a spy movie is seeing all the high-tech vehicles, gadgets, and weapons the agents put to use. Are the high-speed cars equipped with machine guns and the mini-submarines used for underwater escapes realistic, though? How about the microscopic devices that spies plant to eavesdrop on conversations or the miniaturized cameras they use to photograph documents or clandestine meetings?

Some of the high-tech transportation devices are the product of filmmakers' imaginations. However, intelligence agencies such as the KGB spend a great deal of time and money developing gadgets and weapons for their agents to use. One devious KGB device was an umbrella used to kill a Bulgarian anti-communist leader named Georgi Markov in London in 1978. KGB engineers converted the tip of the umbrella into a silenced gun that could fire a poison pellet. A Russian agent "accidentally" brushed against Markov on a London bridge, fired the pellet

into his leg, and then apologized for bumping into him. Markov died mysteriously four days later.

KGB technicians created some other unusual and deadly weapons. One was a cigarette pack adapted to hide a canister of acid. An agent could press a firing device on the outside of the pack to send an acidic spray into a victim's face. By the time the victim fell to the ground, the perpetrator could have easily fled the scene. Another device was a cylinder-shaped gun that could be concealed inside a rolled-up newspaper. Different models of such guns could fire bullets or spray poison gas.

KGB agents using the gas gun were supplied with an antidote to the poison, just in case they accidentally breathed in the gas themselves. Such an antidote was also needed by KGB agents who used a poison-gas firing device hidden in a specially designed wallet. The wallet had an opening out of which the gas could be propelled and a pocket for storing the antidote tablets.

Not all KGB gadgets were designed to kill. Some were created for eavesdropping and photographing. Others were made for hiding and transferring information. One special spy

Some spies carried suppressed (muffled) small-caliber guns, which fire quietly.

A hollowed-out book can make for a safe—and accessible—place to stash a spy's weapon.

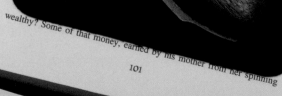

camera could be strapped around an agent's body to take pictures through an opening in a tiepin. Another camera was hidden inside a hollowed-out compartment of a book, its lens pointing through an opening. To take pictures, the spy would press on the book cover and activate a shutter button. Tiny cameras were also sometimes concealed inside briefcases, cigarette packs, wristwatches, and coat buttons.

KGB technicians developed a number of ingenious bugs for recording conversations. One was a pen microphone that could easily fit inside an agent's shirt pocket. Another was an entire recording system concealed in the spine of a book. One of the most famous Russian bugs was actually planted inside the American embassy in Moscow. In 1946, a group of Soviet children presented a two-foot-round (0.6 m) replica of the Great Seal of the United States to U.S. ambassador Averell Harriman. Harriman hung it on the wall behind his desk in Moscow. He never suspected that a special transmitter was hidden inside the seal behind the symbol of a bald eagle. The transmitter was activated

In 1960, the U.S. finally went public with the bugged plaque that had been in its embassy building.

by an outside radio signal. The bug wasn't discovered until 1952, when the U.S. National Security Agency (NSA) was sweeping the embassy for listening devices. It was removed, but its discovery was not made public for several years. Then, in 1960, the U.S. displayed the device before the United Nations (UN) Security Council to demonstrate unethical behavior on the part of the KGB.

One problem that members of all intelligence agencies have is how to best conceal and transfer documents, rolls of film, or microphotographs that contain secret data. KGB technicians created some clever hiding devices that resembled household products such as a hollowed-out shaving cream can or D-cell battery casing or even a hollow iron bolt hammered into a wooden fence. Russian agents also sometimes placed secret information inside metal spikes that had been driven into the ground at a drop.

One of the simplest concealment devices, a hollow American nickel, helped expose a Soviet spy ring operating in the U.S. in the 1950s. In 1953, Jimmy Bozart, a 14-year-old newspaper delivery boy from Brooklyn, New York, accidentally dropped a nickel he had been paid. The coin split in two, and

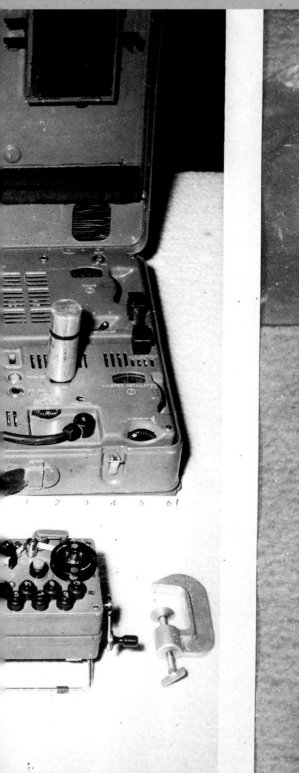

Spies living in other countries could send
messages to Moscow via a radio transmitter.

a microphotograph containing a coded message fell out. Bozart gave the hollow nickel to the police, who then contacted the FBI in New York, but specialists there couldn't break the code. Four years later, the mystery was solved with the help of a Soviet spy who had recently defected. The message provided information about a spy ring led by Soviet illegal Rudolf Abel, who was soon arrested and tried for espionage. The hollow nickel was only one medium Abel's ring used to conceal messages. Members also hid codes and microfilm in hollow cuff links or inside nails they pounded into telephone poles.

While gadgets such as hollow coins or tiepin cameras were needed for spying on the ground, KGB aircraft experts designed different types of satellites, airplanes, and balloons for spying from the sky. In October 1957, the Soviet Union stunned

Opposite: Rudolf Abel was the alias adopted by Vilyam Genrikhovich Fisher upon his 1957 arrest.

people around the world when it launched *Sputnik*, the first man-made satellite. Such artificial satellites opened up new avenues to spies. Now a country's intelligence service could photograph large areas of a foreign country without being detected and then analyze the film for information about military activity. Satellites could also intercept radio communications from the sky. The U.S. was determined to match the Soviet Union and launched its first spy satellite almost four months later.

The more valuable satellites became, the more rigorous was the recruitment of technical and communications experts who could reveal the information they collected. Two Americans who eventually agreed to sell classified information to the Soviet Union were Christopher Boyce and Andrew Lee, known respectively by the nicknames "the Falcon" and "the Snowman." The information they provided alerted the Soviet Union to weaknesses in its own military security and communications. Both young men were eventually caught and imprisoned. Their story is depicted in the 1985 movie *The Falcon and the Snowman*, starring Timothy Hutton and Sean Penn.

SOVIET MASTERS OF DECEPTION

From the 1920s, when Felix Dzerzhinsky headed up the Trust, until the KGB was disbanded in 1991, the directors of Soviet spy agencies were powerful and cruel individuals. Dzerzhinsky formed the Trust to trap anti-communists and ruthlessly eliminated people he thought might threaten the new communist regime. His successor, Vyacheslav Menzhinsky, oversaw the killing of millions of Ukrainian farmers. He was followed by Genrikh Yagoda, who was an expert on poisons and torture. Yagoda was in charge when Stalin ordered the deaths of thousands of communist leaders whom he feared might become powerful enough to rebel against him. Yagoda came under the same suspicion and was so good at his job that Stalin decided to have him killed as well.

Perhaps the most influential Soviet spymaster of all was Lavrenti Beria, who ran the NKVD during and after World War II. It was Beria who sent Soviet agents to penetrate intelligence

agencies and scientific labs in the U.S. and Britain from the 1930s to the '50s. Beria's spies recruited moles in both countries, including several high-ranking leaders of Britain's MI5 (domestic intelligence) and MI6 (foreign intelligence) divisions. They also gathered secrets from both countries that helped the Soviet Union build its first nuclear weapons.

After Stalin died in 1953, Beria believed he would succeed him as leader of the country. Unfortunately for Beria, his rivals had him quickly eliminated. No one is sure just how or by whom. Some people suspect that a rumor about the CIA—

claiming that Beria was one of its assets in the USSR—may have led to the spy's demise.

While Soviet spymasters were known for their outright ruthlessness, Russia's most successful spies were notable for being sneaky and clever. Two Soviet spies who provided valuable information to Moscow during the early days of World War II were Leopold Trepper and Richard Sorge. Trepper was a Polish communist who was brought to Moscow in the mid-1930s for special training. He was then sent to Belgium to set up a spy network that would track the German

Francis Gary Powers, pictured in his flight suit after being captured by the Russians in 1960.

EVOLUTION OF ESPIONAGE
The Spy Swap Bridge

Both sides in the Cold War spent a lot of effort searching for and prosecuting spies. If caught, these spies were often given stiff prison sentences. Later, they might be set free in exchange for the release of a spy from the opposing side. In 1962, for example, Russian spy Rudolf Abel was swapped for an American pilot named Francis Gary Powers, who had flown a spy plane illegally over Soviet air space two years earlier. During the swap, the men passed each other on the Glienicke Bridge between East and West Berlin. That bridge was the site of several other important spy swaps.

Л.П. БЕРІЯ

Lavrenti Beria's espionage against the U.S. and Britain was largely for the Soviet atomic bomb project.

army's movements. Trepper created a fake clothing firm called the Foreign Excellent Raincoat Company to disguise the work of his spy group. When Germany invaded France in 1940, Trepper moved to Paris and contracted with the Germans to provide raincoats for their soldiers. The arrangement allowed the Russian spies to meet with German officers and learn a lot about their plans.

Trepper discovered that Germany planned to invade Russia, even though the two countries were supposed to be allies. At first, Stalin refused to believe the information, but Trepper kept sending more details that finally convinced him. Because Trepper's spy group sent so many radio transmissions to Moscow, the Germans began calling them "the Red Orchestra." The Germans later captured most of the orchestra members, including Trepper. He avoided execution by agreeing to act as a double agent.

However, he worded the messages he sent to Moscow in such a way that the Russians knew they were false. Trepper later escaped and lived out the war in hiding.

Richard Sorge set up a Soviet spy network in Japan just before World War II began. At the time, Stalin was worried that the Japanese might decide to invade Russia from the east. Sorge, who was part German, moved to Tokyo, posing as a German journalist. Through contacts he made, Sorge learned that Japan did not intend to attack Russia. He wanted to relay the news to Moscow right away but had a sense that his radio transmissions were being tracked by the Japanese. Despite the danger, Sorge sent off three long transmissions from a moving sailboat. The information caused great excitement in Moscow. Knowing that their army didn't have to focus on its eastern border enabled Russian generals to send more troops westward to prepare for the German invasion that Trepper had warned was coming. Unfortunately, Sorge's radio transmissions soon led to his capture by the Japanese. First, he was tortured, and then he faced the firing squad.

After World War II ended and the Cold War began, Russian

intelligence agencies focused their efforts on penetrating Western countries such as West Germany, Britain, and the U.S. One man recruited to spy in Germany was a British intelligence officer named George Blake. This double agent revealed a number of key secrets. For example, in 1953, he let the Russians know about a secret tunnel the Americans had built in Berlin for the purpose of tapping phones in Soviet and East German offices. The Russians didn't let on that they knew about the tunnel for three years. In the meantime, they began providing false information on their phones and hoped the

Americans were listening. In 1956, the Russians "accidentally" discovered the tunnel, which was quickly closed down.

The Russians also set up their own spy networks in the U.S. and Britain. The American network was run by KGB colonel Rudolf Abel. One of the men Abel trained was Gordon Lonsdale, whom the Russians then sent to London to establish his own spy ring. Lonsdale's group helped the Soviets discover confidential information about the work of the recently established North Atlantic Treaty Organization (NATO), a military alliance of Western

EVOLUTION OF ESPIONAGE
Telefon

A 1977 spy movie called *Telefon* contained many elements that played on the fears of Americans during the Cold War. In the movie, the Soviet Union has planted sleeper agents in U.S. cities near key military bases, where they are living normal lives. However, if they receive a phone call and hear a special code word, they will be activated and carry out acts of sabotage. A fanatic Russian agent comes to the U.S. and begins making phone calls until he is stopped by another Russian agent. The fact that many Americans believed that sleepers were commonly used made the movie even scarier and more dramatic.

KGB agent Vitaly Yurchenko (on left) faked his defection to the U.S., possibly to protect Aldrich Ames.

countries focused on checking the expansion of Soviet influence and furthering democracy in Europe.

Later in the Cold War, the Russians managed to recruit several moles inside the FBI and CIA. Two of the most infamous were Robert Hanssen and Aldrich Ames. For more than 20 years, Hanssen, whose FBI job was to catch spies, worked undercover for the KGB and SVR. He left dozens of packages containing American intelligence data at drop sites in the Washington, D.C. area. In return, Hanssen was paid more than $600,000 in cash and diamonds—but he ended up serving a lifetime sentence in an American federal prison.

Ames worked as a case officer for the CIA for more than 30 years. Starting in 1985, he began selling secrets to the Russians, receiving payments of more than $2 million. Some of the information Ames provided included names of undercover agents working for the Americans and British inside the Soviet Union. Many of these operatives ended up in Russian prisons or were killed. Ames's spying was finally uncovered in 1994. His arrest sent shock waves through the CIA, and he received life imprisonment.

INSIDE OPERATIONS

Spy missions are designed to obtain inside information—the secrets that others want to keep hidden. Sometimes the best way to do that is to find an insider and win him or her over to your side. That is exactly what Soviet spy agencies did from the 1930s through the 1980s.

The first important mission involved getting inside Britain's main intelligence agencies, MI5 and MI6. The Soviets accomplished this by recruiting five graduates of England's prestigious Cambridge University and encouraging them to join the British government or intelligence services. The "Cambridge Five"—Kim Philby, Guy Burgess, Donald Maclean, Anthony Blunt, and John Cairncross—all belonged to communist organizations in college. They agreed to spy for the Russians largely because of their pro-communist beliefs.

As they rose in the government ranks in the 1940s, two of the Cambridge Five, Philby and

Maclean, were given assignments in the U.S. in which they learned many secrets about the development of the atomic bomb. They passed these along to the Russians. Philby also had access to reports of American efforts to discover which atomic scientists might be revealing secrets of their work to the Russians. He warned the KGB about these reports so that they could protect their assets from being discovered.

Philby was able to keep his spying so secret that he earned promotion after promotion in

MI6 and was in line to become the organization's head in 1951. Then Maclean and Burgess came under investigation for spying and defected to the Soviet Union. Philby was watched carefully after that and decided to join his colleagues in Russia in the early 1960s when it became clear that he too might be arrested. He was later given the rank of general in the KGB. Blunt and Cairncross remained in England. Government leaders kept their spying secret for many years to avoid creating a scandal.

The atomic bomb was the focus of another important Soviet spy mission in the 1940s. The Russians

Opposite: At a November 1955 press conference, Kim Philby declared that he had never been a communist.

were determined to build their own bomb but decided to take a shortcut by stealing secrets from nuclear scientists working on the bomb in America. One scientist more than willing to reveal what he knew was Klaus Fuchs. Fuchs had escaped from Germany before World War II and become a British citizen. Then he came to the U.S. to work on the atomic bomb research team called the Manhattan Project. Like the Cambridge Five, Fuchs was a communist, so he was easy for the KGB to recruit. After the war, Fuchs's spying was discovered, and he was arrested and imprisoned in England.

Fuchs was only one of a number of pro-communists living in the U.S. who conveyed atomic secrets to the Russians during that time. New Yorker Julius Rosenberg and his wife Ethel, whose brother worked on the Manhattan Project, provided atomic bomb details to a Soviet handler in New York. After the Soviets tested their own bomb in 1949, the FBI intensified its efforts to find possible Manhattan

Project leaks. The Rosenbergs were discovered, and they were arrested and later executed for conspiracy to commit espionage.

During the Cold War, both the Russians and Americans concentrated on infiltrating each other's intelligence services. They spent almost as much time trying to discover which of their own intelligence officers might be double agents. One agent who ended up on both sides was Dmitri Polyakov. In 1951, Polyakov was sent to New York as part of the Soviet delegation to the UN. His real purpose was to spy on the U.S., which he did successfully for five years. He returned to the USSR in 1956, then became angry when Russian officials would not let him bring his son to New York for an important medical operation. After the boy died, it is thought that Polyakov blamed his bosses and decided to change sides.

When the KGB sent Polyakov back to the UN in 1961, he offered his services to the CIA. In his double-agent role, Polyakov began sending disinformation to Russia about new chemical weapons the Americans were developing. The CIA hoped the Russians would waste a lot of time and money trying to copy these useless plans. Polyakov worked as a double agent

SEPT. 1950

DR. FUCHS TALKS—AND HUGE SPY-HUNT IS ON

THURSDAY, MARCH 2, 1950

FOR KING AND COMMONWEALTH

NO. 16.782 ONE PENNY

STRUCTURAL ENGINEERS

DOES MY BABY

G-Men and M.I.5

MAR. 1950

Janossy: My place is here

'Happy to serve Hungarians'

From Daily Mail Reporter
VIENNA, Monday.

PROFESSOR Lajos Janossy, the 38-year-old cosmic ray expert from Dublin, who

AUG. 1950

Physicist Klaus Fuchs (bottom, middle) worked on both the British and American atomic projects.

HEBCKИЙ II 4.24 7 962

Dzerzhinsky's fame grew after his 1926 death—so much so that a statue of him was erected in 1958.

HEBCKИЙ II 24 7 962

for more than 20 years until he was exposed by both Robert Hanssen and Aldrich Ames in the 1980s and later executed in Russia.

When the KGB was disbanded in 1991 and replaced by the SVR and FSB, more than just the names changed. So did the types of missions carried out by the two new intelligence agencies. While most spy missions of the NKVD and KGB focused on military secrets, the work of the SVR and FSB is more related to industrial espionage, or spying to learn what new products companies are creating. SVR agents have tried to infiltrate technology laboratories and businesses in countries such as Germany, Israel, China, and South Korea, as well as the U.S., to learn about new types of computers, aircraft, cars, and robots. SVR computer experts have also hacked into the systems of important technology companies to learn more secrets. Why the focus on industrial espionage? Russian government and business leaders believe Russian companies can save a lot of money developing new products if they have inside information. One German expert estimates that Russian spies steal up to $5 billion in industrial secrets from Germany each year and

EVOLUTION OF ESPIONAGE
Bringing Back the Statue

When the KGB attempt to take over the Russian government failed in 1991, many angry Russians marched on the agency's headquarters in Lubyanka Square (which had previously been named Dzerzhinsky Square for the first Soviet spymaster). The crowd pulled down a giant iron statue of Dzerzhinsky to show their contempt for the repressive ways of the KGB. Soon the organization was broken apart to form the SVR, FSB, and several smaller agencies. In recent years, however, Russian leaders have proposed replacing the statue on its base near the FSB's offices. Does this mean that the KGB is returning to power? Most Russians hope not.

EVOLUTION OF ESPIONAGE
High Price for a Spy

During the 22 years FBI agent Robert Hanssen served as a Russian mole, he was paid more than $600,000 for spying. According to a 2002 book written by espionage author David Wise, the FBI paid an SVR agent $7 million for information that led to Hanssen's arrest. The book is entitled *SPY, The Inside Story of How the F.B.I.'s Robert Hanssen Betrayed America*. Wise wrote that the SVR agent turned over a suitcase full of evidence that never mentioned Hanssen's name but provided clear hints to his identity. Hanssen was arrested in February 2001 while leaving a garbage bag full of classified information at a park near Washington.

billions more from other countries. Meanwhile, the FSB has increased its counterespionage efforts to make sure that Russian technology secrets are not likewise revealed to other countries.

Russian prime minister Vladimir Putin, a former KGB chief, has told the Russian people that the SVR is a very different organization from earlier Russian intelligence agencies. The old agencies were designed to repress Russians' human rights, Putin said, while the new ones are charged with defending democracy in Russia. Are the days of terror tactics by the Russian secret police truly over? Are dissidents in Russia no longer under threat of being exiled to Siberia? It is not easy to tell because the new Russian agencies are determined to keep their work secret from the eyes of outsiders. Russia, the world's largest country in total area, remains one of the most unknowable. We may never uncover its deepest mysteries on our own, but perhaps there are some things best left undisturbed.

Above: Vladimir Putin served as Russia's second president (2000–08) before becoming its prime minister.

ENDNOTES

agents—people who work for, but are not necessarily officially employed by, an intelligence service

assets—hidden sources acting as spies or providing secret information to a spy

bugs—electronic listening devices that usually contain a microphone, transmitter, and antenna

Cold War—the hostile competition between the United States and its allies against the Soviet Union and its allies that began at the end of World War II and lasted until the collapse of the Soviet Union in 1991

communist—one who supports a political and economic system in which all goods and property are owned by the state and shared by all members of the public

defect—in the context of spying, to choose to leave the control of one country's intelligence service to work for another country; defectors often provide vital information to their new country

deported—forced to leave a foreign country and return to one's own country

dictatorship—rule by strong and often cruel leaders who have absolute power

disinformation—false or misleading intelligence, often provided by double agents

dissidents—people who disagree with and rebel against a government

double agents—spies for one country who double as spies for a second country and often provide false information to the first country

drop—a secure location that usually includes a sealed container where spies and their handlers can exchange information or intelligence materials to avoid meeting in person

embassy—the headquarters of an ambassador and staff in a foreign country

intelligence officers—people who gather or distribute information uncovered and transmitted by spies

nuclear weapons—bombs, rockets, and other weapons that cause destruction as a result of a nuclear explosion

operatives—undercover agents working for an intelligence agency

surveillance—watchful observation of suspicious people

tradecraft—the procedures, techniques, and devices used by spies to carry out their activities

treason—the crime of betraying one's country

tsar—a Russian emperor before 1917

WEB SITES

Language of Espionage
http://www.spymuseum.org/kids-language-espionage
Familiarize yourself with all the terms a good spy should know.

Notorious Russian Spies throughout History
http://www.time.com/time/photogallery/0,29307,2000712_2159099,00.html
Check out this photo essay from *TIME* to see pictures of famous spies.

SELECTED BIBLIOGRAPHY

Andrew, Christopher, and Oleg Gordievsky. *KGB: The Inside Story*. New York: HarperCollins, 1990.

Bledowska, Celina, and Jonathan Bloch. *KGB/CIA: Intelligence and Counterintelligence Operations*. New York: Exeter Books, 1987.

Crowdy, Terry. *The Enemy Within: A History of Espionage*. Oxford: Osprey Publishing, 2006.

Earnest, Peter, and Suzanne Harper. *The Real Spy's Guide to Becoming a Spy*. In association with the International Spy Museum. New York: Abrams, 2009.

Mahl, Tom E. *Espionage's Most Wanted: The Top 10 Book of Malicious Moles, Blown Covers, and Intelligence Oddities*. Washington, D.C.: Brassey's, 2003.

Owen, David. *Spies: The Undercover World of Secrets, Gadgets, and Lies*. Buffalo, N.Y.: Firefly Books, 2004.

Volkman, Ernest. *Spies: The Secret Agents Who Changed the Course of History*. New York: John Wiley & Sons, 1994.

Yost, Graham. *The KGB: The Russian Secret Police from the Days of the Czars to the Present*. New York: Facts on File, 1989.

INDEX